DEFEATING EPILEPSY WITH EXPERT GUIDANCE

Ultimate Solution Handbook For Patients, Guardians Or Family To Understand, Manage, Treat, Prevent, Reverse Symptoms And Live Well

DR. POTTER WHITLEY

Copyright © 2023 by Dr. Potter Whitley

DISCLAIMER:

This book's contents are meant to be used solely for informative purposes. The information should not be used as a replacement for expert medical advice, diagnosis, or care.

The information contained in this book is accurate and reliable, having been verified by the author to the best of his ability. Nevertheless, the author disclaims all express and implied representations and warranties regarding the availability, correctness, appropriateness, completeness, and reliability of the material provided here. You bear full responsibility for any reliance you may have on such material.

For informational purposes, this book may make reference to or mention of certain people, things, websites, organizations, or other names. The author has no connection to, endorsement from, or recommendation for these organizations. The author's approval or validation is not implied by the inclusion of these references.

Any direct, indirect, incidental, special, or consequential damages resulting from using or not being able to use the material in this book are not covered by the author's liability policy. For medical advice and counsel particular to their circumstances, readers are advised to check with experienced healthcare specialists.

The content, materials, and information in this book are subject to change at any time without prior notice, at the author's discretion. The text may contain errors or omissions for which the author is not responsible.

By reading this book, you understand and accept the conditions of this disclaimer.

THE REASON BEHIND THIS BOOK

"Defeating EPILEPSY With Expert Guidance" is an extensive and priceless resource that sheds light on the intricate world of epilepsy and gives readers a thorough understanding of the illness. Chapter 1 of this book provides an in-depth analysis of the basics of epilepsy, including an informative introduction, a look at the many kinds of seizures, a determination of the causes and triggers, and a consideration of how epilepsy affects day-to-day living. This basis gives readers a comprehensive understanding that is essential for understanding the following chapters.

Building on this framework, Chapter 2 explains the intricate scientific details of epilepsy. This book offers a thorough examination of the science underlying epilepsy, covering everything from the neurological causes of the disorder to the function of brain structure and genetics. In Chapter 3, the nuances of the diagnostic process are explained, enabling readers to understand the significance of consulting neurologists and epilepsy specialists for professional assistance. Diagnostic instruments and tests are also deconstructed. This section advocates for a collaborative healthcare strategy that guarantees a thorough comprehension of the condition's diagnosis and testing.

This book deftly transitions into Chapter 4, which examines a range of treatment alternatives, including prescription drugs, surgery, alternative therapy, and lifestyle changes. This comprehensive approach reaffirms the goal of this book to offer a comprehensive manual for managing epilepsy. As they go along, readers learn how important it is to have a strong support network, which is covered in Chapter 5. Stressing the interdependence of a holistic approach, the significance of family and friends, support groups, mental health considerations, and teaching others about epilepsy are emphasized.

In-depth methods for controlling stress, identifying triggers, and encouraging a healthy lifestyle are covered in Chapters 6 and 7. Readers learn how to identify stressors, develop coping strategies, practice relaxation, and understand the importance of proper diet, exercise, sleep hygiene, and substance usage. The book deftly moves between general parts on epilepsy in children, epilepsy with pregnancy, and the changing field of developing technology and research. These chapters provide focused insights that address several facets of managing epilepsy, including the particular difficulties moms and children encounter.

Furthermore, Chapter 11's personal triumph tales enhance the story by offering hope and motivation. These stories emotionally connect with readers because they emphasize perseverance, the strength of support, and overcoming obstacles. This book skillfully blends scientific understanding with personal experience to provide a comprehensive manual that inspires and informs readers as they embark on their quest to overcome epilepsy. "Defeating EPILEPSY With Expert Guidance" is a priceless tool that bridges the knowledge gap between medical professionals and those who are affected by epilepsy.

TABLE OF CONTENT

CHAPTER ELEVEN 98

[11]

CHAPTER ONE

AN OVERVIEW OF EPILEPSY
Overview of Epilepsy

The neurological condition known as epilepsy is typified by frequent, erratic seizures that arise from aberrant electrical activity in the brain. People of all ages, genders, and origins are impacted by this illness, which makes it a serious public health concern. There are several ways in which seizures can appear, from brief loss of consciousness to spasms involving the entire body. The frequency of epilepsy emphasizes how crucial it is to comprehend its causes, manifestations, and potential effects on a person's life.

Disturbances in the regular neural activity pattern cause epileptic seizures, which are characterized by abrupt and transient alterations in behavior, awareness, and sensation. Epilepsy is a complex and heterogeneous disorder because of the considerable variation in the frequency and severity of seizures among affected individuals. Given that people with epilepsy frequently experience difficulties in their social and personal lives, it is critical to understand that epilepsy is a chronic condition requiring ongoing care and assistance.

Seizures' Types:

Different types of epileptic seizures can be distinguished according to their features and the parts of the brain that are affected. Seizures classified as focal (partial) and generalized are the two primary types. Different symptoms may arise from focal seizures based on the exact area of the brain that is affected. Uncontrollable movements, altered emotions, and sensory abnormalities are a few possible signs. Abnormal activity in the brain occurs during generalized seizures, which usually cause convulsions, loss of consciousness, and other extensive repercussions.

Various distinct kinds of seizures fall under these broad categories, including absence seizures, myoclonic seizures, atonic seizures, and tonic-clonic seizures. Every variety has distinct difficulties and factors to be taken into account for both epileptics and those who support them. Comprehending the unique attributes of every seizure variety is crucial for precise diagnosis, therapeutic interventions, and seizure management.

Reasons and Initiators:

Many different factors can contribute to epilepsy, such as brain trauma, infections, genetics, developmental disorders, and structural abnormalities in the brain. When the precise etiology of epilepsy cannot be determined, the condition is categorized as idiopathic. Furthermore, epileptics may experience seizures in response to certain triggers. Stress, sleep deprivation, flashing lights, certain medications, and drug or alcohol abuse are a few examples of these triggers.

Effective management and treatment of seizures depend on determining their underlying cause as well as any potential triggers. To identify the cause and customize interventions to the patient's requirements, a thorough medical evaluation that includes imaging studies and neurological tests is frequently required. Healthcare providers can help people manage their epilepsy and enhance their general quality of life by treating the underlying causes and reducing triggers.

Effects on Day-to-Day Living:

Epilepsy can have a substantial impact on a range of daily activities, including social interactions, emotional health, work, and education. Seizures can be unpredictable, making it difficult to stick to a schedule and take part in activities that other people might take for granted. Some of the challenges that people with epilepsy may encounter are social stigma, restricted educational opportunities, and employment discrimination.

Epilepsy is typically managed with a mix of medication, lifestyle changes, and coping mechanisms. Maintaining a regular medication regimen is essential for controlling seizures; however, managing side effects and the requirement for continuous medical supervision may make treatment more challenging. Adjustments and safety precautions may need to be taken due to the possibility of seizure activity during routine tasks like driving or taking a bath.

It's important to recognize the emotional toll that epilepsy can have since it can cause social isolation, anxiety, or depression in some people. Getting support from friends, family, and medical professionals is essential when dealing with the psychological and emotional effects of having epilepsy. Increasing knowledge and comprehension about epilepsy within communities can help to lessen its stigma, promote inclusivity, and make the environment more accepting of those who are impacted by the condition.

To sum up, epilepsy is a neurological condition that is complex and necessitates a thorough understanding of its nature, seizure types, underlying causes, and the significant impact it can have on day-to-day living. People with epilepsy can benefit from specialized support and interventions to improve their general well-being and manage the difficulties brought on by their condition by addressing these factors under the direction of a professional.

CHAPTER TWO

THE NATURE OF EPILEPSY SCIENCE
The Neural Underpinnings Of Epilepsy:

The complex neural networks of the brain are the source of epilepsy, a neurological condition marked by recurrent seizures. The brain is a multifaceted organ made up of billions of connected neurons that exchange signals chemically and electrically. This complex system undergoes aberrant electrical activity bursts in epilepsy, which results in seizures. These aberrant electrical discharges can happen in particular brain regions, and each person will experience seizures differently.

Investigating how neurons interact and maintain the delicate balance of excitatory and inhibitory signals is crucial to understanding the neurological underpinnings of epilepsy. Changes in this equilibrium may lead to hyperexcitability, which in turn creates the ideal environment for seizures.

Neurotransmitters that are important in preserving this balance include glutamate and gamma-aminobutyric acid (GABA). Seizures result from neurons that are more likely to fire excessively when this balance is upset.

The significance of anatomical anomalies in the brain has also been brought to light by research on the neurological underpinnings of epilepsy. Areas of increased excitability caused by lesions, tumors, or scars from injuries can serve as focal points for epileptic activity. Epilepsy can also arise as a result of changes in ion channel function, which controls the passage of ions across neuronal cell membranes.

Through deciphering the complex neurological mechanisms that underlie epilepsy, scientists hope to create focused therapies that can adjust brain activity and lessen seizure frequency. Modern neuroimaging methods, like functional and magnetic resonance imaging (MRI), have shed light on the anatomical and functional characteristics of the brain and made it easier to pinpoint regions that are more likely to experience epileptic seizures.

Anatomy of the Brain and Epileptic Behavior:

One of the most important aspects of comprehending and treating epilepsy is the relationship between brain anatomy and epileptic activity. The human brain is a very well-organized structure with different regions handling different tasks. Unusual electrical activity in epilepsy frequently stems from particular brain regions, resulting in seizures with a variety of clinical presentations.

Anomalies in particular brain structures are closely linked to focal epilepsy, a condition in which seizures start in a restricted area of the brain. For example, the hippocampus, frontal lobe, and temporal lobe are frequently locations linked to focal epileptic activity. The onset of seizures is influenced by disruptions in the normal functioning of these structures, which are crucial for memory, emotions, and motor functions.

Furthermore, the idea of the "epileptic focus" highlights a brain focal point that serves as the starting and spreading point for aberrant electrical discharges. It is essential to comprehend the anatomical features of these epileptic foci to plan the appropriate course of treatment. Clinicians can now identify the precise brain regions implicated in epileptic activity and pinpoint structural abnormalities thanks to high-resolution imaging technologies like magnetic resonance imaging (MRI) and computerized tomography (CT) scans.

Functional connectivity within the brain's networks is a significant factor influencing epileptic activity, independent of structural abnormalities. Conditions that are favorable for seizures can be produced by abnormalities in the communication between various brain regions. Technological developments in neuroimaging, such as magnetoencephalography (MEG) and electroencephalography (EEG), have improved our capacity to record and examine the dynamic interactions between different brain regions during epileptic episodes.

Creating focused therapeutic interventions requires an understanding of the complex interactions between brain anatomy and epileptic activity. Medical practitioners can strive toward more efficient seizure management techniques by customizing treatments to address particular anatomical abnormalities and functional disruptions.

Genetic Elements:

The complex interaction between genetic predisposition and environmental factors in the development of epilepsy is clarified by the role of genetic factors in this neurological disorder. A significant percentage of epilepsy cases can be linked to inherited factors, even though not all cases have a clear genetic cause.

In terms of its genetic foundation, epilepsy can be divided into two main categories: idiopathic and symptomatic. Idiopathic epilepsy suggests a strong genetic component, where seizures occur without an apparent cause or associated neurological abnormalities. On the other hand, symptomatic epilepsy indicates that seizures result from identifiable brain lesions or structural abnormalities, often with a genetic basis.

Research has found multiple genes involved with diverse kinds of epilepsy, regulating parameters such as ion channel function, neurotransmitter modulation, and neuronal growth. Mutations in these genes can disturb the delicate balance of excitatory and inhibitory signals in the brain, resulting in an increased susceptibility to seizures.

Understanding the genetic mechanisms contributing to epilepsy has substantial implications for both diagnosis and therapy. Genetic testing can assist in identifying individuals at risk for hereditary forms of epilepsy, enabling early intervention and individualized treatment regimens. Moreover, as our understanding of the genetic basis of epilepsy grows, researchers are pursuing gene treatments and precision medicine approaches to target specific genetic defects and control their impact on neuronal function.

In addition to inherited genetic variables, de novo mutations—genetic abnormalities that develop spontaneously—also play a role in epilepsy. These mutations can affect normal brain development and increase the chance of seizure activity. The intricate interplay between genetic predisposition and environmental factors further complicates the terrain of epilepsy research, underlining the necessity for thorough investigations that examine both genetic and environmental influences.

Diagnostic Tools and Tests:

Accurate and fast diagnosis is important in managing epilepsy effectively, and developments in diagnostic tools and testing have changed our ability to diagnose and understand this neurological illness. A multi-faceted strategy, integrating clinical assessments, imaging technology, and electrophysiological research, plays a crucial role in reaching a full diagnosis.

Electroencephalography (EEG) stands as a cornerstone in the diagnostic armament for epilepsy. By recording the brain's electrical activity through electrodes placed on the scalp, EEG records the unique patterns linked with seizures. Continuous EEG monitoring, especially in the form of long-term video EEG, allows clinicians to correlate clinical symptoms with specific electrographic anomalies, aiding in the classification of seizure types and diagnosis of epileptic syndromes.

Imaging methods such as magnetic resonance imaging (MRI) and computed tomography (CT) have considerably expanded our ability to visualize structural abnormalities in the brain. With the use of these non-invasive methods, precise images can be obtained, which aid in the identification of lesions, tumors, or other abnormalities causing epileptic activity. More thorough knowledge of the neural underpinnings of epilepsy is made possible by advanced imaging methods such as positron emission tomography (PET) and functional magnetic resonance imaging (fMRI). These procedures provide insights into the dynamic functional characteristics of the brain.

Apart from the traditional diagnostic methods, genetic testing has become an effective means of determining the hereditary causes of epilepsy. Molecular genetic testing facilitates a more accurate diagnosis and helps guide treatment choices by identifying certain gene alterations linked to epilepsy syndromes. Genetic testing is becoming a crucial component of the diagnosis process as our knowledge of the genetic variables impacting epilepsy expands, particularly in situations where a hereditary component is suspected.

The development of artificial intelligence (AI) has also had a major impact on diagnosing epilepsy. Clinicians can receive assistance from machine learning algorithms that have been trained on large datasets of EEG recordings in detecting minor patterns and anomalies that may be invisible to human observers. These AI-powered diagnostic tools have the potential to increase the efficiency and precision of epilepsy diagnosis, which will ultimately result in more individualized and focused treatment plans.

To sum up, the continuous progress in comprehending the neurological foundation of epilepsy, the complex connection between brain structure and epileptic activity, the influence of hereditary elements, and the changing range of diagnostic instruments and assessments all add up to a more sophisticated and efficient method of treating this intricate neurological ailment. There is still hope for better diagnosis and individualized treatment plans for people with epilepsy as long as research yields new knowledge and technological advancements.

CHAPTER THREE

GETTING EXPERT ASSISTANCE
Why Medical Consultation Is Important

Getting expert assistance is crucial for managing epilepsy. An organized and knowledgeable strategy for comprehending and treating this neurological condition is offered by medical consulting. It is the first step toward a successful course of therapy and a better quality of life for those who have epilepsy.

The comprehensive evaluation carried out by medical specialists is one of the most important components of medical consultation. Clinicians can learn vital information about the unique features of each patient's epilepsy through comprehensive medical histories, neurological tests, and talks regarding the frequency and kind of seizures.

When creating a treatment plan that takes into account the particular requirements and difficulties that every patient has, this information is priceless.

Additionally, getting a medical consultation guarantees that people are informed accurately about their illness. Patients and their families must be aware of the type of epilepsy, its triggers, and lifestyle changes. With this information, people are more equipped to take an active role in their care and develop appropriate management techniques for their epilepsy.

Monitoring the course of treatment is also greatly aided by routine visits with medical personnel. Changes in seizure patterns or the emergence of new adverse effects may need modifications to medication or other measures. People with epilepsy can confidently and with help negotiate the complexities of their condition by keeping lines of communication open with medical specialists.

In conclusion, medical consultation is crucial to treating epilepsy because it serves as a basis for individualized care, a source of information for patients and their families, and a means of continuous monitoring and plan modifications.

<u>Experts In Neurology And Epilepsy:</u>

In the fight against epilepsy, neurologists and epilepsy experts play a crucial role. Their proficiency with the subtleties of epilepsy and the intricacies of the neural system is essential for a precise diagnosis and efficient treatment of the ailment.

As medicine specialists, neurologists offer a thorough understanding of the brain and its operations. They are essential in determining the precise kind of seizures a person with epilepsy has. Neurologists can identify the brain regions implicated in seizure activity via thorough examinations and, if necessary, advanced imaging techniques including EEGs (electroencephalograms) and MRIs (magnetic resonance imaging).

On the other hand, doctors who have focused their knowledge exclusively on the study and treatment of epilepsy are known as epilepsy specialists.

These experts can offer targeted and nuanced treatment because they frequently have a great deal of expertise in managing a range of seizure diseases. They make sure that their patients have access to the most cutting-edge and successful solutions by staying up to date on the most recent research and developments in the treatment of epilepsy.

One major advantage in the fight against epilepsy is the collaborative nature of neurologists and epilepsy experts. Together, they can combine their expertise and viewpoints to produce more thorough treatment regimens and precise diagnoses. This comprehensive approach guarantees that people with epilepsy receive the best possible therapy by addressing both the underlying causes of their condition and any current symptoms.

In summary, the ability of neurologists and epilepsy experts to navigate the intricacies of epilepsy—from

precise diagnosis to customized treatment regimens—
is crucial to the eventual objective of curing epilepsy.

Procedure for Diagnosis and Testing:

Epilepsy diagnosis is a laborious and important process that includes several tests and evaluations to precisely determine the kind and underlying causes of seizures. This all-encompassing method is crucial for creating a successful treatment plan and improving the general quality of life for epileptics.

The electroencephalogram is one of the main diagnostic instruments for epilepsy (EEG). This non-invasive technique captures brain electrical activity and assists in identifying aberrant patterns linked to seizures. Long-term or continuous EEG monitoring can yield useful information by catching elusive seizure occurrences that may not be seen during shorter examinations.

Neuroimaging methods like magnetic resonance imaging (MRI) are frequently used in addition to EEGs. With the use of MRIs, medical professionals can see the anatomy of the brain and identify any anomalies that might be causing seizures. This can include growths, wounds, or other anatomical abnormalities that might point to a neurological disease.

Another crucial step in the diagnosis process is genetic testing, particularly when there is a possibility that the epilepsy has a genetic component. Knowing the genetic components involved can help guide treatment choices and give patients and their families important knowledge about the inherited basis of the illness.

There is no "one size fits all" method for the diagnostic process. It necessitates carefully evaluating a person's medical history, seizure characteristics, and test results. Putting this complicated puzzle together requires the cooperative efforts of neurologists, epilepsy specialists, and other medical professionals.

To sum up, epilepsy testing and diagnosis require a multifaceted approach that makes use of cutting-edge technologies and teamwork to precisely determine the kind and cause of seizures. This accuracy is essential for creating customized treatment programs and eventually achieving the goal of curing epilepsy.

The Collaborative Healthcare Method:

To successfully treat epilepsy, a multidisciplinary team approach to treating the many facets of this intricate neurological condition is necessary. Individuals with epilepsy will receive comprehensive care that addresses the medical, psychological, and social aspects of their condition thanks to this team-based approach.

In the collaborative healthcare approach, allied health professionals such as nurses, psychologists, neurologists, and epilepsy specialists are usually involved. Every team member contributes a different set of abilities and knowledge, which helps to create a comprehensive picture of each person's requirements and difficulties.

Key players in this collaborative strategy, neurologists and epilepsy experts concentrate on the medical aspects of epilepsy. They determine the kind of seizures, pinpoint the underlying reasons, and recommend the right drugs or other treatments. To modify treatment regimens according to the patient's response and changing condition, regular coordination and communication between these professionals is essential.

To provide continuing assistance and education, nurses are essential. They offer advice on how to track seizures, manage medications, and change one's lifestyle. Additionally, by treating the emotional and social effects of epilepsy, psychologists and social workers contribute. They help people negotiate cultural stigma or constraints and cope with psychological issues that may develop.

The collaborative approach involves active participation from individuals with epilepsy and their families in addition to healthcare professionals. This paradigm fosters resilience and a sense of agency by giving people the power to actively participate in their care.

To summarize, overcoming epilepsy requires a coordinated healthcare approach that takes into account the condition's complex character. Through the integration of diverse specialized knowledge and active engagement with persons and their support networks, this strategy optimizes the likelihood of effective management and enhanced quality of life.

[37]

CHAPTER FOUR

AVAILABLE THERAPIES
Drugs Used to Treat Epilepsy:

The use of antiepileptic drugs is a fundamental component of epilepsy treatment. These medications are essential for managing and preventing seizures, which improves the quality of life for those who have epilepsy. The kind of seizure and the patient's general condition are typically taken into consideration while choosing the right medicine.

Antiepileptic medications function by reducing aberrant neuronal firing that causes seizures by regulating the electrical activity in the brain. But it's important to remember that different people react differently to different medications, which emphasizes the value of a customized approach to epilepsy treatment.

There are numerous classes of antiepileptic drugs, each having a distinct mode of action and possible adverse effects. Among the medications that are frequently prescribed include lamotrigine, phenytoin, carbamazepine, and valproic acid.

The kind of epilepsy, age, gender, and the existence of other medical disorders all influence the treatment selection. To minimize side effects and for optimal seizure control, regular monitoring and dosage modifications may be required.

Successful therapy depends on patients following the recommended medication schedule, and medical professionals frequently collaborate closely with patients to resolve any questions or problems regarding their medications.

Some people may have drug-resistant epilepsy, which is characterized by seizures that continue even after trying several antiepileptic medications. In these situations, other therapeutic options, like as surgery and complementary therapies, might be investigated to enhance overall quality of life and seizure control.

Surgical Procedures:

Surgical procedures present a potential path for improving seizure management and, in certain situations, establishing complete seizure freedom for persons with drug-resistant epilepsy. During epilepsy surgery, the part of the brain that causes seizures is removed or altered. Making the difficult decision to have surgery is usually the result of a comprehensive assessment by a multidisciplinary team that includes neurologists, neurosurgeons, and neuropsychologists.

Temporal lobectomy, in which part of the temporal lobe is removed, and corpus callosotomy, in which the nerve fibers between the brain's two hemispheres are destroyed, are common surgical operations for epilepsy. Respondent neurostimulation is an additional choice in which an apparatus is inserted into the brain to identify and stop aberrant electrical activity.

dangers are associated with surgery, therefore it's important to weigh the advantages against the dangers. While some patients have notable improvements in their quality of life and ability to control their seizures after surgery, others might not experience the same degree of benefit. To evaluate the success of the procedure and handle any possible complications, postoperative care, and continuous monitoring are crucial.

Alternative Medical Interventions:

Complementary options for managing epilepsy are increasingly examining alternative therapies in addition to traditional medical and surgical approaches. These treatments cover a wide range of techniques, such as biofeedback, acupuncture, herbal supplements, and dietary changes. While there is conflicting scientific data about the effectiveness of these alternative medicines, some people may benefit from using them in addition to conventional treatments.

The ketogenic diet, a high-fat, low-carb diet that has demonstrated promise in lowering seizures, particularly in children with epilepsy, is one well-known alternative therapy. Although the precise processes by which the ketogenic diet reduces seizure activity are not entirely known, it is thought to do so by changing the brain's metabolism.

Before implementing alternative therapies into their epilepsy management strategy, those thinking about them should speak with their healthcare practitioners. The safe and successful integration of alternative therapies is ensured by a collaborative and educated decision-making process that considers the patient's health status, treatment objectives, and potential interactions with other interventions.

Changes in Lifestyle:

In addition to pharmaceutical and surgical treatments, lifestyle changes are essential for improving general health and managing epilepsy. Keeping a regular sleep pattern is essential since sleep disruptions can cause seizures in certain people. Better sleep quality can be attributed to practicing adequate sleep hygiene, which includes establishing a calming bedtime routine and reducing screen time before bed.

An epilepsy management plan may benefit from the inclusion of stress-reduction strategies such as deep breathing exercises, mindfulness meditation, and consistent physical activity. Adopting stress-reduction techniques may help to improve seizure management as chronic stress has been identified as a potential seizure cause.

Apart from managing stress, it's crucial to steer clear of recognized triggers for seizures, like heavy alcohol intake and specific drugs. It is suggested for people with epilepsy to consume alcohol in moderation or not at all since it can reduce the seizure threshold and interfere with the effectiveness of antiepileptic medications. Being aware of one's triggers and making wise lifestyle decisions enable people to actively control their epilepsy.

It is essential to have routine medical check-ups with healthcare professionals to assess the efficacy of the selected treatment methods, make any drug adjustments, and handle any new issues. Through a comprehensive and individualized strategy that integrates medication, surgical interventions, alternative therapies, and lifestyle modifications, people with epilepsy can overcome the obstacles presented by this neurological disorder and achieve a full life.

[45]

CHAPTER FIVE

BUILDING A SUPPORT SYSTEM
Family and Friends' Role in Defeating Epilepsy With Expert Guidance

In the battle against epilepsy, friends and family play a crucial role. As a neurological condition, epilepsy impacts the sufferer directly and also has an impact on those in their immediate social circle. Family and friends' emotional and psychological support can make a big difference in an epileptic person's overall well-being.

Families are essential in providing a secure and compassionate atmosphere for people with epilepsy. Family members must comprehend the basics of seizures, including their nature, potential triggers, and how to react in an emergency. Family members can help manage epilepsy efficiently in the long run by becoming knowledgeable about the condition and being able to act immediately after a seizure.

Furthermore, emotional assistance is essential. People who have epilepsy may experience discrimination and stigma, and friends and family can serve as a buffer against such prejudice. Families with open lines of communication enable members to voice their hopes, frustrations, and anxieties, creating a supportive and understanding atmosphere for the epileptic member.

Friends are essential in building a network of support as well. Social connections are essential for mental health, and friends can be sources of support through trying times. Comprehending the friend's medical condition and any particular requirements they might have, such as avoiding certain situations or knowing when to take their medications, makes the friendship more inclusive and encouraging.

Essentially, the role that friends and family play goes beyond providing urgent care during seizures; it also includes fostering an atmosphere of understanding, compassion, and unwavering support. Family and friends become essential members of the person's support network by actively participating in the road to overcoming epilepsy, which promotes resilience and improved mental health.

Communities and Support Groups in Overcoming Epilepsy With Professional Advice

Communities and support groups are vital tools in the fight against epilepsy because they offer a sense of acceptance and comprehension that is frequently hard to find elsewhere. These communities provide a platform for people to share stories, exchange information, and gain strength from the collective knowledge of those who are living with epilepsy, which may be an isolated experience.

Being a part of a support group can be very powerful since it encourages people to share their success stories and coping mechanisms. People who have epilepsy frequently confront comparable obstacles, therefore it can be instructive to hear about other people's experiences navigating similar circumstances. Support groups serve as a useful resource for handling the day-to-day challenges of living with epilepsy in addition to providing emotional support.

These networks also offer a forum for awareness-raising and advocacy. Together, people who have epilepsy and those who support them can battle stigma, spread knowledge about the condition, and build a more accepting society. A support group's combined voice can have a significant impact on legislative changes, healthcare access, and the advancement of medical research for better treatment alternatives.

In particular, online communities have grown to be vital for bringing people together who live in different parts of the world. These platforms facilitate instantaneous connection, cultivating an international support system. People with epilepsy feel more united when they share information about new research, treatment alternatives, and emotional support, which cuts across national boundaries.

In summary, communities and support groups have a variety of roles to play in the process of overcoming epilepsy. They are essential parts of the support network for people with epilepsy because they offer emotional support, useful guidance, and a forum for activism.

Taking Into Account Mental Health Issues When Fighting Epilepsy With Professional Advice

Since epilepsy affects not only physical but also mental and emotional health, treating mental health issues is essential to winning the battle against the disorder. Since social isolation, melancholy, and anxiety are common issues for people with epilepsy, it is critical to include mental health support in their overall care plan.

Seizures can be unpredictable, which can make people more anxious. The constant fear of the next seizure can have a profound effect on one's mental health. Because of this, a thorough strategy for controlling epilepsy needs to incorporate anxiety-reduction tactics including mindfulness, relaxation techniques, and, in certain situations, therapeutic interventions.

Another prevalent mental health issue among epileptics is depression. The chronic nature of the illness and any restrictions it may place on day-to-day activities might exacerbate depressive and dismal feelings. By including mental health specialists on the care team, people may be sure they are getting the emotional support and treatments they need to deal with their depression.

Because epilepsy is stigmatized, social isolation is a recurrent problem for many people with the condition. Withdrawing from social interactions out of fear of criticism or misunderstanding can hurt mental health. This isolation can be fought and a healthy mental outlook can be fostered by encouraging social inclusion and creating supportive conditions within communities.

Furthermore, it is impossible to ignore how epilepsy affects cognitive performance. The illness itself may cause memory problems and cognitive difficulties, or pharmaceutical side effects may occur. To overcome these obstacles and improve cognitive capacities, neuropsychologists' assistance and cognitive rehabilitation may be essential.

In summary, overcoming epilepsy necessitates a comprehensive strategy that gives mental health issues a priority. Through the treatment of anxiety, depression, social isolation, and cognitive difficulties, people with epilepsy can improve their overall quality of life and develop resiliency against this neurological disorder.

Teaching People About Epilepsy and Helping Them Beat It With Professional Advice

In the fight against stigma and false information, educating people about epilepsy is essential. There are many misconceptions regarding epilepsy, which contribute to prejudice, social exclusion, and ignorance. Thus, spreading accurate information throughout communities and increasing awareness are crucial to ending epilepsy.

Dispelling misunderstandings about epilepsy should be the first step in epilepsy education. Many individuals continue to have antiquated ideas about the origins and characteristics of seizures, which feeds misinformation and anxiety. People may help to remove these obstacles and create a supportive and empathetic environment by disseminating correct information.

Moreover, it's critical to raise knowledge about first aid protocols for seizures. Due to ignorance, many individuals pause or behave inappropriately when they see someone having a seizure. By providing basic first aid knowledge, communities can be better equipped to respond to seizures and lessen the potential harm that may occur during an episode. These skills include creating a safe atmosphere, timing seizures, and providing assistance afterward.

Communities, businesses, and educational institutions can all be vital hubs for epilepsy education. Awareness campaigns, educational meetings, and training courses can all contribute to the development of a welcoming environment where people with epilepsy feel supported and accepted. This helps create a more understanding and knowledgeable society in addition to helping people who are directly impacted by epilepsy.

Apart from official educational programs, anecdotes can serve as an effective means of enhancing comprehension. To personalize the experience and dispel misconceptions, people who have personally experienced epilepsy or who have close relationships with someone who does can share their tales.

In summary, spreading awareness of epilepsy is crucial to overcoming the obstacles brought on by this neurological condition. A supportive and inclusive environment for people with epilepsy can be created by individuals and groups by debunking myths, advancing first aid skills, and cultivating an empathetic culture.

CHAPTER SIX

HANDLING STRESS AND TRIGGERS
Identifying Stressors

An essential component of successfully controlling epilepsy is identifying stresses. Seizures can vary greatly in frequency and intensity depending on stress. Everybody has different stressors, therefore it's important to know what personally triggers you. Emotional stressors like worry, despair, or extreme enthusiasm are common, as are physical stressors like sleep deprivation, exhaustion, or disease. Stressors in the environment, such as bright lights or loud noises, can potentially trigger seizures. Hormonal fluctuations and specific drugs can also be stressful for some people. Acknowledging these pressures necessitates self-awareness and frequently entails maintaining a thorough seizure journal to monitor possible trends and triggers over time.

It's critical to distinguish between typical stresses and those that are specifically associated with seizures when managing epilepsy. Stress in daily life is unavoidable, but acute or chronic stress that has a direct impact on seizure activity requires special consideration. While some people may not see a clear association, others may notice an increase in seizures during times of increasing stress. Stressor awareness enables people to proactively reduce their effects, laying the groundwork for improved epilepsy care.

Coping Strategies:

Coping strategies are essential for overcoming the difficulties posed by epilepsy. Since seizures are unpredictable, learning useful coping mechanisms is crucial to preserving general well-being. People who adopt a holistic perspective might integrate emotional and psychological coping strategies into their everyday routines. Therapy sessions, mindfulness exercises, and cognitive-behavioral strategies can help people learn more effective coping mechanisms for stress and anxiety, which lowers the risk of seizures.

Creating a solid support network is another essential coping strategy. Support networks such as family and friends can provide both practical and emotional support, promoting resilience in the face of epilepsy-related difficulties. Advocacy groups and educational materials can also offer insightful knowledge and a feeling of belonging. Positive coping strategies can include taking initiative, defining reasonable objectives, and acknowledging minor successes.

Methods of Relaxation:

Relaxation methods reduce stress and enhance general well-being, making them useful tools in the management of epilepsy. People can become calmer by using methods like progressive muscle relaxation, guided visualization, and deep breathing techniques. Including these exercises in regular routines improves the person's capacity to handle stress and lowers the risk of seizures.

Because it promotes increased awareness of the present moment, mindfulness meditation in particular has shown promise in the management of epilepsy. By encouraging people to notice their thoughts and feelings without passing judgment, mindfulness practices help people become more resilient and in charge of their lives. Regular relaxation training not only helps people feel less stressed but also develops a more optimistic outlook, which is good for their general health and helps them control their seizures.

Recognizing and Steering Clear of Triggers

Being aware of and steering clear of triggers is a proactive way to manage epilepsy. There is a great deal of variation in triggers, thus identifying them needs a careful examination of lifestyle and surroundings. A regular sleep schedule is vital because for certain people, sleep deprivation or irregular sleep patterns may function as triggers. Some individuals can discover that specific meals, drugs, or hormonal fluctuations affect the frequency of their seizures. Furthermore, as was already said, stress can be a major trigger for a lot of people.

Once triggers are recognized, avoiding them becomes an essential part of day-to-day living. This could entail dietary alterations, pharmaceutical adjustments, or lifestyle changes made under a doctor's supervision. Modifications to the surroundings, such as reducing exposure to bright lights or loud noises, may also be important. Important elements of this process include education and self-awareness, which enable people to make well-informed decisions about their everyday activities and choices. This, in turn, improves seizure control and promotes overall well-being.

CHAPTER SEVEN

LEADING A WELL-BEING LIFE
Epilepsy And Nutrition:

Epilepsy management is greatly influenced by nutrition, and controlling seizures can be greatly impacted by eating a balanced diet. Although there isn't a single "epilepsy diet," several nutritional strategies, including the ketogenic diet, have shown promise in helping some people experience fewer seizures. A high-fat, low-carb diet called the ketogenic diet encourages ketosis, which may change how the brain uses energy and lessen seizure activity. Furthermore, regular, well-balanced meals might assist in maintaining stable blood sugar levels, preventing swings that could cause seizures. Furthermore, since dehydration might make seizures more likely, it's critical to maintain adequate water.

There is evidence linking some micronutrients, like magnesium and vitamin B6, to the regulation of seizures. It may be advantageous to include foods high in these nutrients, such as seafood, almonds, and leafy greens. However, it's best to stay away from such triggers as overindulging in alcohol or coffee. A licensed dietician can offer individualized advice and make sure that dietary decisions are in line with a person's unique health requirements and seizure patterns.

Physical Activity And Exercise:

Frequent physical activity is beneficial not just for general health but also for the management of epilepsy. Exercise improves mood and sleep quality, lowers stress, and supports cardiovascular health—all of which can have an impact on seizure control. Some people with epilepsy can engage in more strenuous activity, but others may need to take into account their restrictions and choose low-impact activities like walking or swimming.

Exercise causes the production of endorphins, which enhance well-being and may aid in the management of stress, a major seizure trigger. Developing a regular exercise regimen that includes both strength training and aerobic activities might improve general health and perhaps lower the frequency of seizures. Before beginning any new fitness program, it is imperative to speak with medical professionals because every person is different and has different seizure triggers.

Suitable Sleep Position:

Good sleep is essential for everyone, but it's especially critical for those who have epilepsy. Seizures can occasionally be brought on by sleep deprivation and abnormal sleep patterns. Developing healthy sleeping habits can make a big difference in how well seizures are managed. This entails keeping a regular sleep schedule, setting up a cozy sleeping space, and abstaining from stimulants like caffeine right before bed.

Making relaxation methods a priority, such as deep breathing exercises or meditation, might improve the quality of sleep, lower stress levels, and possibly lessen the likelihood of seizures. In addition, establishing a peaceful evening ritual and reducing screen time before bed might help the body recognize when it is time to wind down and facilitate the transition to sound sleep. A key component of managing epilepsy is determining and treating any underlying sleep abnormalities, such as sleep apnea.

Epilepsy And Drug Use:

Drug use must be closely monitored when managing epilepsy since some drugs might worsen seizures or reduce the efficacy of prescribed treatments. For example, alcohol can raise the risk of seizures and reduce the seizure threshold. People who have epilepsy must limit their alcohol use or, in certain situations, abstain from it completely.

Similarly, antiepileptic medicines (AEDs) may interact adversely with recreational substances and some prescription pharmaceuticals. Individuals must have open communication with their healthcare professionals regarding any medications or substances they may be taking to verify that their epilepsy treatment plan is compatible. Smoking may carry additional dangers, particularly for people using

AEDs. Therefore, attempts to minimize or eliminate smoking can help improve general health.

For those who have epilepsy, education, and knowledge of the possible hazards related to substance use are essential. Maintaining open lines of communication with medical professionals enables the creation of individualized treatment plans that take into account each person's unique requirements and sensitivities, improving general health and seizure control.

CHAPTER EIGHT

EPILEPSY IN CHILDREN
Overview of Childhood Epilepsy:

Childhood epilepsy is a neurological condition that affects children from birth through adolescence and is typified by repeated seizures. The aberrant electrical activity in the brain that causes these seizures manifests itself in a variety of ways, both physically and behaviorally. Beyond only the seizures, epilepsy affects a child's overall quality of life, scholastic performance, and cognitive development. Understanding the various symptoms of pediatric epilepsy and its possible causes, such as genetics, brain trauma, or infections, is vital for parents and other caregivers.

Effective management of infantile epilepsy requires early diagnosis. When doing thorough assessments, which include neurological examinations, medical histories, and diagnostic procedures like brain imaging and electroencephalograms (EEGs), pediatric neurologists are essential.

The ability to recognize distinct seizure types and patterns facilitates the customization of treatment regimens to meet the individual requirements of every child. Furthermore, for comprehensive care, it is essential to take into account the possible effects of epilepsy on cognitive and emotional development.

Children with epilepsy encounter difficulties in their academic pursuits, social interactions, and emotional health. To promote inclusivity and understanding, epilepsy education is necessary in communities and schools. Additionally, the field of treating pediatric epilepsy is still being shaped by continuing research and breakthroughs in treatment options, which gives affected children hope for better outcomes and an improved quality of life.

Approaches to Pediatric Treatment:

A comprehensive strategy is used to treat pediatric epilepsy with the goals of reducing side effects, managing seizures, and enhancing general well-being.

Antiepileptic drugs are recommended based on the particular type of seizure and the child's reaction. They are frequently regarded as the first line of defense. The necessity of close observation to modify drug dosages and handle possible adverse effects highlights the significance of cooperation between pediatric neurologists, parents, and caretakers.

Medication alone may not be enough to manage seizures in certain kids. Alternative therapies such as neurostimulation techniques or ketogenic diet therapy may be taken into consideration in such circumstances. For certain people, the high-fat, low-carb ketogenic diet has been demonstrated to be effective in lowering seizures. By using tools to alter brain activity, neurostimulation provides a non-pharmacological method of controlling seizures.

When various treatments fail to control seizures, surgical intervention may be considered. Respective surgery or the installation of a neurostimulator are two possible surgical interventions. A careful analysis of the advantages and disadvantages of surgery must be made, necessitating cooperation between the child's family and the medical staff.

Counseling and behavioral treatments are examples of complementary therapies that are essential parts of all-encompassing care. Pediatric epilepsy therapy is ensured by a holistic strategy that strikes a balance between the medical components of treatment and the child's psychological requirements.

Advocacy and Support from Parents:

The diagnosis of epilepsy in a child has a profound impact on the individual as well as parents and other caregivers. Getting a child with epilepsy well means handling their medicine, arranging doctor's visits, and helping them deal with the emotional toll that the disorder has on the family. In addition to advocating for their child's medical needs, parents frequently find themselves serving as community educators and ambassadors for epilepsy.

Beyond the necessities of medical care, parental support includes helping the child develop resilience, self-worth, and independence. A supportive atmosphere where the child feels understood and empowered to manage their illness is fostered by open communication within the family. Parent-focused education programs can give parents the information and abilities they need to deal with the difficulties of parenting an epileptic kid.

More broadly, advocacy includes debunking misconceptions and lowering stigma related to epilepsy. To encourage more knowledge and understanding, parents should work with advocacy groups, take part in neighborhood activities, and share their personal stories. By raising their voices, parents help create a more accepting community that enables kids with epilepsy to realize their full potential.

Making the Move to Adulthood:

For those with epilepsy, the shift from youth to adulthood is a crucial time that comes with special difficulties and responsibilities. Young people with epilepsy frequently experience changing medical, educational, and social demands as they get older, which calls for careful consideration and preparation. To address the evolving dynamics of managing epilepsy and to ensure continuity of care, pediatric neurologists and healthcare professionals are essential.

During the transition period, medical issues include reassessing drug adherence, monitoring potential side effects, and reevaluating treatment strategies. Establishing a thorough adult treatment plan, discussing the patient's history, and transferring medical data all depend on clear communication between pediatric and adult healthcare providers. By bridging the gap between childhood and adult epilepsy care, this partnership guarantees that each person's specific needs are satisfied as they grow into adulthood.

Transitions in education are similarly significant since young adults with epilepsy could need modifications in contexts such as higher education or the workplace. People can be empowered to pursue their academic and professional aspirations by advocating for educational support and raising knowledge of their legal rights.

Furthermore, encouraging self-reliance and self-advocacy abilities equips young individuals to actively manage their epilepsy as they negotiate the challenges of adulthood.

The social and emotional components of living with epilepsy as an adult include dealing with relationships, mental health, and self-worth. Young adults with epilepsy may benefit from peer support groups, counseling programs, and community resources as helpful networks to assist them in dealing with potential social issues. A successful transition is facilitated by resilience building and positive self-image encouragement, which enable people to live satisfying lives despite the difficulties presented by epilepsy.

CHAPTER NINE

EPILEPSY AND PREGNANCY
Handling Epilepsy In A Pregnant Woman:

Pregnancy-related epilepsy management is a sensitive and complicated process that needs to be carefully thought out to protect the developing fetus as well as the mother. Due to the possibility of hormonal changes, stress, and sleep disturbances during pregnancy causing seizures, women with epilepsy have particular hurdles. The main objective is to strike a balance between reducing potential dangers to the developing baby and effectively managing seizures.

A key component of treating epilepsy during pregnancy is teamwork between the obstetrician, neurologist, and patient. The neurologist is essential in modifying antiepileptic drug dosages to achieve a fine balance between seizure control and preventing possible fetal damage. It is imperative to closely monitor seizure activity throughout pregnancy and make necessary adjustments to medication dosages to ensure optimal seizure control.

It's crucial to remember that abruptly stopping antiepileptic drugs can be dangerous because uncontrollably occurring seizures can endanger both the mother and the developing fetus. As a result, any modifications to medicine must be properly thought out and carried out under the supervision of medical specialists. To evaluate the efficacy of the treatment plan and swiftly address any new concerns, patients and healthcare practitioners must maintain regular check-ups and communication.

During pregnancy, lifestyle changes can also help treat epilepsy in addition to medication treatment. Reducing stress, getting enough sleep, and leading a healthy lifestyle all improve general well-being and may lessen the likelihood of seizures. To support both their health and the health of the growing baby, women with epilepsy are frequently encouraged to follow a well-balanced diet, use relaxation techniques, and maintain a regular sleep routine.

In summary, treating epilepsy during pregnancy necessitates a thorough and customized strategy that takes into account the particular requirements of each patient. For women with epilepsy, a successful and healthy pregnancy can be facilitated by regular communication between the lady and her medical team, diligent seizure monitoring, and appropriate medication modifications.

Considerations for Medication:

Pregnancy-related epilepsy management requires careful assessment of drug options, as the need to keep the mother's seizures under control must be carefully balanced with the possible effects on the growing fetus. The main treatment for seizures is the use of antiepileptic medicines (AEDs), and decisions about their usage during pregnancy need to be well-thought-out and well-informed.

The possible teratogenic effects of several AEDs, which raise the possibility of congenital abnormalities in the growing fetus, are an important factor to take into account. Healthcare professionals must carefully weigh the benefits and hazards of each medicine, including things like the woman's epilepsy type, history of seizures, and any effects on fetal development.

In certain circumstances, it could be able to change the AED being used or modify the dosage if it has a better safety record for pregnancy. However, to make sure that the woman's ability to regulate her seizures is not jeopardized, such decisions need to be taken in cooperation with an obstetrician and neurologist.

The timing of medication modifications is also very important. To reduce any hazards to the developing fetus, drug regimen adjustments are frequently undertaken before conception or in the early stages of pregnancy. Uncontrollable seizures might result from abrupt adjustments or stopping AED use, which puts the mother and unborn child in danger.

To make sure that therapeutic levels are maintained throughout pregnancy, drug levels must be continuously monitored. This entails routine blood testing and necessary dosage modifications for medications. Finding the ideal balance between reducing any hazards to the fetus and effectively controlling her seizures is a dynamic process that calls for constant cooperation between the woman's medical team and herself.

In conclusion, women with epilepsy must carefully weigh the potential hazards and benefits of taking medication during their pregnancy. This is a complex balancing act. Making educated decisions, implementing individualized treatment programs, and closely monitoring the mother are all essential to guaranteeing the health of the growing fetus.

Prenatal Treatment for Moms with Epilepsy:

The goal of comprehensive and specialized prenatal treatment for women with epilepsy is to protect the developing fetus's health while optimizing the health of the mother. Because epilepsy presents special problems, neurologists and obstetricians must carefully coordinate to offer individualized care that takes into account the demands of pregnancy as well as seizure management.

A vital component of prenatal treatment for mothers with epilepsy is early and frequent contact with medical professionals before conception. This makes it possible to thoroughly evaluate the woman's medical background, frequency of seizures, and antiepileptic drug schedule. To achieve the best possible seizure control and reduce any dangers to the developing fetus, medication adjustments may be taken into consideration before conception.

Frequent prenatal exams are necessary to assess the mother's and the unborn child's health during pregnancy. Specialized procedures, like non-stress tests and fetal ultrasounds, may be performed at these visits to evaluate the health of the growing fetus. Women with epilepsy may be more susceptible to complications, so it's especially critical to monitor for conditions like preeclampsia.

Throughout the pregnancy, the woman and her medical team must maintain close communication. This covers continuing talks about controlling seizures, managing the woman's medication, and any new issues or changes to her health. Antiepileptic medication changes may be required in specific circumstances; the neurologist and obstetrician should collaborate on these decisions.

Prenatal care for moms with epilepsy involves lifestyle variables in addition to medical considerations. Overall well-being is influenced by leading a healthy lifestyle that includes frequent exercise, a balanced diet, and stress reduction. For women who have epilepsy, getting enough sleep is especially crucial because sleep disturbances may result in seizures.

To sum up, prenatal treatment for moms with epilepsy entails a multidisciplinary approach that takes into account the particular requirements of pregnancy as well as the special difficulties associated with epilepsy. For women who are managing their epilepsy, regular communication, early planning, and continuous monitoring are key components of a successful and healthy pregnancy.

Postpartum Concerns:

For women who have epilepsy, the postpartum phase presents particular challenges because of the fluctuating hormone levels and possible sleep disturbances that may affect seizure activity. Neurologists, obstetricians, and other healthcare professionals must work together to manage postpartum care for women with epilepsy to facilitate a seamless transition into motherhood and maintain the best possible seizure control.

Resuming antiepileptic medication after delivery is one immediate consideration. Under the supervision of a neurologist, it is imperative for women who temporarily modify their pharmaceutical regimen during their pregnancy to revert to their pre-pregnancy plan.

This procedure is usually started soon after delivery to reduce the possibility of postpartum seizures.

Monitoring for any possible issues relating to epilepsy or childbirth is another aspect of postpartum care. Given that the postpartum phase can be difficult for any new mother, medical professionals keep a close eye on the woman's general health, particularly her mental health. For women with epilepsy, postpartum care must include mental health support, including screening for postpartum depression.

Many new mothers worry about breastfeeding, and women with epilepsy might wonder if it's safe to breastfeed while using antiepileptic drugs. Most of the time, nursing and some antiepileptic drugs work well together, but it's important to talk about this with medical professionals so that you can make decisions that take the needs of your infant's nutrition and your health into account.

It is crucial to keep an eye on seizure activity after giving birth because the early postpartum period's hormonal changes and sleep disturbances might affect how frequently seizures occur.

To guarantee rapid response, healthcare providers should be informed of any changes in seizure patterns or worries about medication side effects.

CHAPTER TEN

RESEARCH AND EMERGING TECHNOLOGIES
Progress in the Study of Epilepsy:

Recent years have seen incredible advancements in the study of epilepsy, with several ground-breaking findings that have greatly expanded our knowledge of this neurological condition. The development of neuroimaging technologies, such as positron emission tomography (PET) and functional magnetic resonance imaging (fMRI), has allowed scientists to learn more about the complex processes occurring in the brain during epileptic episodes. These developments have led to new understandings of the underlying mechanics of epilepsy in addition to increased diagnostic accuracy.

The genetic components influencing an individual's susceptibility to epilepsy have been identified thanks in large part to genetic studies. Personalized treatment options have been made possible by the identification of specific gene mutations associated with different forms of epilepsy by scientists thanks to the development of high-throughput genomic sequencing. Moreover, developments in molecular biology have illuminated the complicated interactions between ion channels and neurotransmitters, revealing the intricate network dynamics that cause epileptic seizures.

Modern treatments for epilepsy, such as neurostimulation, have gained promise in addition to conventional medication approaches. Targeted control of abnormal neuronal activity is made possible by devices like responsive neurostimulation (RNS) and deep brain stimulation (DBS), which offer a more individualized and successful therapeutic strategy. These developments target the wider range of cognitive and affective elements of epilepsy in addition to seizure management.

Artificial intelligence (AI) research collaborations have produced prediction models that can predict epileptic occurrences based on patient-specific data. Electroencephalogram (EEG) data patterns are analyzed by machine learning algorithms to enable early identification and prompt action. Because they allow for tailored preventive efforts, these prediction models hold the potential to completely transform the management of epilepsy.

These developments have the potential to launch a new age of individualized and targeted therapy as we continue to work across disciplines to understand the complexity of epilepsy. The combination of genetics, neuroimaging, and novel therapeutic approaches portends a more thorough knowledge of epilepsy and, as a result, more successful management techniques.

Creative Methods of Treatment:

The field of treating epilepsy has changed dramatically as a result of the advent of novel strategies that go beyond conventional pharmaceutical treatments. A notable development is in the field of neuromodulation, where tools like deep brain stimulation (DBS), vagus nerve stimulation (VNS), and responsive neurostimulation (RNS) have shown promise in treating drug-resistant epilepsy.

Targeted neural circuit modification is a key component of neurostimulation treatments, which control aberrant brain electrical activity. For example, VNS stimulates the vagus nerve with electrical impulses, which modulates extensive brain networks implicated in seizures. RNS, on the other hand, provides a customized and flexible therapy strategy by identifying aberrant electrical patterns and providing response stimulation to stop the onset of seizures. DBS, a well-proven method for treating movement disorders, has demonstrated potential in treating epilepsy by applying electrical stimulation to particular brain areas linked to the production of seizures.

The discovery of innovative antiepileptic medicines (AEDs) that target particular biochemical pathways linked to seizure activity has also markedly advanced pharmacotherapy. A more individualized strategy has emerged with the advent of precision medicine, in which drug selection is guided by genetic profiles to maximize effectiveness and minimize negative effects. Furthermore, studies on the use of cannabinoids, specifically cannabidiol (CBD), have shown promise in lowering the frequency of seizures, providing a therapy option for patients who might not respond to traditional methods.

The therapy of epilepsy has given rise to the recognition of complementary and alternative therapies. Dietary approaches like the ketogenic diet and mindfulness-based interventions have demonstrated promise in lowering seizure frequency and enhancing general well-being. These all-encompassing methods emphasize how crucial it is to take into account the complex nature of epilepsy and implement an all-encompassing treatment plan.

The integration of these various treatment approaches is crucial to improve outcomes for people with epilepsy as we navigate this innovative period. A change toward more individualized and efficient epilepsy care is seen in the customization of interventions to the unique requirements and features of every patient.

Prospects for Epilepsy Management in the Future:

Driven by continued research, technological improvements, and a better understanding of the underlying mechanics of the condition, the future landscape of epilepsy care holds intriguing promises. Genetic profiling will likely play a key part in personalized medicine, directing treatment plans to optimize benefits and reduce side effects. Big data and artificial intelligence combined will improve prediction models even further, enabling earlier detection of epileptic episodes and more accurate forecasting.

With the development of closed-loop systems that can dynamically adapt to an individual's neural activity, neurostimulation technologies are set to advance. For example, responsive neurostimulation (RNS) devices may advance in their capacity to identify minute modifications in brain activity, allowing for preventive treatment before the manifestation of overt seizures. A departure from conventional open-loop methods, closed-loop systems provide a more flexible and individualized method of managing epilepsy.

The development of tailored drug delivery systems, which would enable the exact administration of antiepileptic drugs directly to afflicted brain regions, holds promise for the use of nanotechnology advancements. The goal of this focused strategy is to reduce systemic adverse effects while increasing therapeutic efficacy. Additionally, studies into the neuroprotective qualities of specific substances may result in the creation of therapies that lessen the long-term emotional and cognitive effects of epilepsy in addition to controlling seizures.

The discipline of regenerative medicine offers the chance to fix damaged brain circuits that are connected to epilepsy. For example, stem cell therapies provide a new way to treat the underlying causes of epilepsy by potentially replacing or regenerating damaged neurons. Though research in this area is still in its infancy, regenerative medicine offers a revolutionary strategy that may one day completely change how we understand and manage epilepsy.

Looking ahead, utilizing the full potential of these developing technologies will require interdisciplinary collaboration. A collaborative strategy involving neuroscientists, geneticists, engineers, and data scientists will guarantee that advances are converted into useful and efficient treatments for people with epilepsy. With focused, individualized, and comprehensive interventions, epilepsy therapy has the potential to improve the overall quality of life in addition to managing seizures in the future.

Clinical Trial Participation by Patients:

The advancement of epilepsy research and therapy is largely dependent on the active involvement of epileptics in clinical studies. In addition to being a basic ethical need, patient participation in these studies is essential to guaranteeing the creation of safe and efficient therapies. Clinical trials offer a forum for investigating cutting-edge therapeutic modalities, evaluating new medications, and improving our knowledge of epilepsy.

Access to state-of-the-art treatments that may not be provided by normal care is one of the main advantages of patient involvement in clinical trials. Clinical trials look into novel drugs, equipment, or therapies that could have a big influence on how epilepsy is managed. For those who take part, this is an opportunity to get new and possibly more effective medicines while also advancing medical science.

Beyond the personal advantages, clinical trial participation adds to the body of information about epilepsy research. Researchers can obtain important information on the safety, effectiveness, and tolerance of therapies across a range of demographic groups by enrolling a diverse participant pool. The presence of diversity in the study sample improves the generalizability of the results, making them more relevant to a wider range of epileptic individuals.

Additionally, clinical trial participation by patients promotes cooperation between scientists and the epilepsy community. To make sure that the interests and preferences of people with epilepsy are taken into account when setting research priorities, collaboration is crucial. Patient feedback can influence research designs, outcome measures, and clinical trial management in general, leading to more pertinent and patient-centered studies.

Improving patient recruitment and retention in clinical trials requires addressing potential obstacles to participation, such as lack of knowledge, logistical difficulties, or safety concerns. Initiatives for education that give precise and understandable information on the goals, methodology, and possible advantages of clinical trials can enable people with epilepsy to make well-informed decisions about taking part.

In summary, the active participation of epileptics in clinical trials is essential to the continuous advancement of knowledge about and interventions for this intricate neurological condition. By taking part in these studies, people not only have access to cutting-edge therapies but also make a collective contribution to the advancement of medical knowledge and the betterment of epileptic populations in the future. The involvement of patients in clinical trials is still essential to bring about significant improvements in the treatment and management of epilepsy as science continues to advance.

CHAPTER ELEVEN

INDIVIDUAL TRIUMPH STORIES
Motivational Stories:

Those who suffer from epilepsy, a neurological condition characterized by recurring seizures, frequently face great difficulties. Despite the stigma and doubts, there are inspiring accounts of people who, with the right help, have overcome epilepsy. These stories are inspirational lights that shine on the route ahead of those who are traveling a similar path.

Sarah's tale is one such instance; she was given an epilepsy diagnosis at a young age. At first, the unpredictable nature of her seizures clouded her goals. However, Sarah was able to identify her triggers and properly manage her condition with the help of skilled medical personnel. She became a champion for epilepsy awareness after transforming her diagnosis from a source of weakness into a source of power.

These accounts demonstrate the bravery and resiliency of those who deal with epilepsy. By talking about their experiences, individuals not only give themselves more confidence but also build a community of support that helps to break the stigma attached to the illness. The tales end up serving as a monument to the human spirit's capacity to overcome hardship, giving hope to those who might be facing comparable difficulties.

Overcoming Obstacles:

Overcoming epilepsy is a series of struggles against mental and physical obstacles rather than a straight line. Professional assistance is essential for people to overcome these obstacles and succeed. Take Michael's narrative, for example, who, despite opposition from the general public due to misunderstandings regarding epilepsy, found comfort and fortitude under the care of an experienced neurologist.

Along the way, Michael had to overcome the psychological effects of stigma in addition to managing the physical aspects of his seizures.

Through the guidance of a compassionate healthcare provider, he fostered resilience, created coping mechanisms, and gradually tore down the walls that epilepsy had built around him. Overcoming obstacles required a multifaceted strategy, and professional advice served as Michael's compass as he navigated the intricacies of his illness.

These tales highlight the fact that beating epilepsy means more than just avoiding seizures—it means conquering all of the challenges that come with the condition. Professional advice turns into a vital ally, giving the means and tactics required to face and overcome the various obstacles that crop up during this life-changing adventure.

The Strength of Willpower and Encouragement:

The road to overcome epilepsy is characterized by the unwavering strength of determination and support. Think about Emily's experience, where a network of relatives, friends, and medical experts came together to support her. This network of support turned into a vital asset in her fight against epilepsy, providing solace in times of need and acknowledging each little accomplishment.

Emily's progress was driven by her determination and the help of experts. She adopted a resilient mindset, changed her lifestyle, and undertook strict treatment regimens. Emily was strengthened by the unfailing support of those around her, which created a synergy that kept her strong in the face of hardship.

These stories emphasize the mutually beneficial interaction that exists between encouragement, willpower, and professional advice. Turning the defeat of epilepsy into a shared victory is not a solo endeavor but rather a team effort. People can endure through the most difficult parts of their condition because of the powerful force that is human connection.

Optimism for the Future:

In the field of expertly guided epilepsy defeat, success tales open doors to a better future. These stories offer the larger epilepsy community as well as the individual hope they convey. People like Sarah,

Michael, and Emily sow hope for others who are still battling the disorder's shadows by sharing their triumphs.

Guidance from experts is essential to fostering this hope. Future developments in medical research could lead to even more potent treatments and better quality of life for those who suffer from epilepsy. This is made possible by the insights offered by experienced healthcare experts. The combined victories presented in these stories serve as arrows pointing the way toward a day when epilepsy will have less of an impact and people will be able to live more fulfilled lives without limitations.

In the end, the success stories of individuals who have overcome epilepsy highlight the significance of a supportive community, the ability of professional advice to bring about transformation, and the human spirit's tenacity. By commemorating these tales, we not only remember past triumphs but also foster optimism for the future, encouraging others to set out on their adventures with grit and hope.